100 INDOOR GAMES for PRESCHOOLERS

A room full of preschoolers means a room full of energy. This book is loaded with games that will help you use that energy to praise God and learn more about His love. Just a quick look through these fresh game ideas will make planning a time with preschoolers easy for any setting—home, school, church, anywhere! And keep one of these little books handy for those times when you need an on-the-spot idea.

100 INDOOR GAMES FOR PRESCHOOLERS

Cook Ministry Resources
a division of Cook Communications Ministries
Colorado Springs, Colorado/Paris, Ontario

© 1997 Cook Ministry Resources
a division of Cook Communications Ministries
4050 Lee Vance View
Colorado Springs, CO 80918-7100

All rights reserved. Except for brief excerpts for review purposes, no part of this book may be reproduced or used in any form without written permission from the publisher.

Editor: Janna McCasland
Designer: Sonya Duckworth

Printed in the United States of America
ISBN: 0-7814-5330-5

CONTENTS

Getting to Know You 1-11
Bible Stories 12-38
Bible Times 39-53
Family Fun 54-63
All About Church 64-75
Character Builders 76-89
Happy Holidays 90-100

GETTING TO KNOW YOU

1 *I Spy a Special Person*

Play a version of "I Spy" called "I Spy a Special Person." When playing this game, children can highlight positive features about other children such as hair color, eye color, clothing. The leader demonstrates by saying something like "I spy a special person who is wearing blue stripes." The children can raise their hands to guess who the special person is. The child who guesses correctly gets to be the next one to choose the special person. Each child should be chosen at least once as you emphasize that God has made everyone wonderful and unique.

2 *What's My Name?*

Sitting in a circle, children say their own name aloud just before rolling the ball to another person in the circle. Encourage them to make eye contact so that they will know when they will be receiving the ball. The game may be played again later with the child calling the name of another child in the circle before rolling the ball to that person. This will introduce them to the group and help them to learn the names of other children.

3 Meet My Friend

Here is a game that will help children become better acquainted. Hide pairs of different colored happy faces around the room. When the leader says "GO!" the children search for one face. When two children find the same color they become partners. They are then to find out their partner's name and favorite animal. When the group comes back together, each child can introduce his or her partner.

4 Group Hug!

Play music as children move around the room. Direct their movement with directions such as tip-toe, skip, hop, crawl, etc. When the music stops, each child finds someone to hug, saying "Jesus loves you!" Repeat with instructions for groups of three to hug, then four, etc. The kids may make a new friend as they share Jesus' love through hugs!

5 Touch That Color!

This game is another opportunity for children to get to know each other and to remind them of all the fun colors that God has made. Place children in pairs or small groups. The leader calls out, "Touch something red (or another color)!" and each child must touch a piece of their partner's clothing that is the color the leader called out.

6 *Name Game*

This simple rhythm game will help children to learn each other's names and become more comfortable with new friends.

Have children sit in a circle and establish a simple rhythm by patting thighs and clapping alternately, or by patting knees alternately. Once the rhythm is established, all chant together: "I have a good friend, _____ is his/her name," with children taking turns filling in their names until everyone has been introduced.

Variation for older preschoolers: As the children become more confident, you might have each individual recite these two lines in rhythm: "My name is _____, and my eyes are _____." (or, "and my hair is _____," or "and I like _____"); then the rest of the class echoes the lines back to the child who first recited them. ("Her name is Karen, and she likes spaghetti.")

7 *Stumped!*

To help children learn the names of the others in their group, have everyone sit in a circle. Go around the circle and have each child tell his or her first name. After the child says his or her name, the group must think of an action that starts with the same sound as the child's name (e.g. Jim—jump, Laquisha—laugh, Marissa—mop). The leader may have to help the kids identify the first sound in the name before they can think of an action. The child must then do that action. If the group is stumped and can't think of an action to go with the name, everyone in the group must roll up in a ball like a tree stump, and say, on the count of three, "We're stumped!"

8 *Color Match*

This matching game will help kids get moving among other children while working on recognizing their colors and shapes. In advance, cut out pairs of shapes from different colors of construction paper. Be sure that every shape has a match (both color and shape should be the same.) Tape the shapes to the backs of half the kids and tell the kids that they cannot take them off or look at them. Give the other shapes to kids and allow them to look at them. They must then go and find the child who has the shape that matches theirs—tell them to make sure both the shape and the color are the same. When a child thinks that he or she has found a matching shape, that child and the child with the match should walk over to a designated wall. They can then take the shape off the back of the child, make sure it really is a match, and then hold the shapes up in front of them. If the children decide that the two really don't match exactly, they should place one of the shapes on the child's back again and return to the group to find the correct pairs. If the shapes do match exactly, the pair should stand together, holding up their shapes until everyone has found their match.

9 *Animal Intro*

Children sit in a circle. Each chooses an animal that he or she would like to be. Each child needs to choose a different animal so that no children have the same animal name. Then have them choose and demonstrate a motion for their animal (arm as trunk for elephant, wag hand as a tail for dog, clap hands together for crocodile, etc.). Go around the circle and have each child tell the name of their animal and demonstrate their animal's motion. The leader starts the game by making his or her own animal motion and then the animal motion of another person. That person must then make his or her motion and another. If a child gets stumped and can't think of another animal motion, or does not make his or her own animal motion first, that child must get up and walk one time around the outside of the circle, making the motions and sounds of his or her animal. That child then sits back down in the circle and the person to his or her left starts play again by making his or her own animal motion and then one of another child in the group.

10 *Name Train*

The leader begins this game by going up to a child and saying, "Name train, name train, what's your name?" The child answers, telling the leader his or her name. The leader then repeats the child's name, imitating the way it was said (Loud or soft voice, accent, etc.), "Jesse... Jesse, Jesse-Jesse-Jesse." (This can get fun when the children realize you will imitate the way they say their name!) That child then stands behind the leader with his or her hands on the leader's waist forming the beginning of the Name Train. The child that is now part of the train joins the leader in asking the children their names and repeating the names as they are said. Each child is added to the back of the train until everyone is part of the name train. Encourage the children to wrap the train around each child as they ask him or her to join the train so that the child feels welcomed by all and so that the people at the back of the train remain just as much a part of the game as those at the front.

11 *Name Tug-of-War*

Divide the group into two teams. Have all the members of both teams stand in a circle around a pillow. Each child should hold onto a part of a pillow. (If there are too many kids to hold onto one pillow, divide them again and have some play a second round.) At the leader's signal, the children must pull the pillow over a designated point for their team. The team that wins the tug-of-war gets to go first in the "naming" part of the game. For this part of the game, the two teams are to line up facing each other. The team that won the tug-of-war should start the game by saying the name of one of the kids on the opposite team. Have the teams go back and forth saying the name of one person on the other team. The teams are not allowed to repeat someone's name for more than one turn. The team that knows the most names of kids on their opposing team wins. Mix the children up, divide them into new teams, and play again. Soon the kids will know all the names of those in their group!

BIBLE STORIES

12 Grape Mania

The story from Matthew 21:28-32 is about a father who asks his two sons to help him work in the vineyard, but only one son obeys his father. For a fun game to go along with this story, label two cardboard boxes with the word "grapes." Prior to the game, have all the children crumple up more than enough pieces of paper to fill both boxes. Place all the crumpled "grapes" in one spot, some distance from the boxes and divide the group of children into two teams. At the leader's signal, have each team work together to try to fill their team's box first.

13 Remember the Lord's Supper

Have the children sit in a circle around a tablecloth set with the following items: place mat, napkin, cup, plate, round loaf of bread, juice pitcher. The children should cover their eyes while the child who is "It" removes one item from the tablecloth and moves the remaining items around. The children can then uncover their eyes, and the first child to raise his or her hand and guess the missing object becomes "It." The game is over when all the items have been removed or each child has been "It." Remind the group that Jesus ate the Lord's Supper with His disciples (Luke 22:14-20) and asked them to remember Him each time they ate this special meal.

14 *David's Not Afraid!*

Children love to play games relating to the courage that God gave David in facing Goliath! Have children crouch on the ground with one student, selected to be David, holding 5 clumps of loosely wadded newspaper where Goliath can't see them. Another student, selected as Goliath, walks among the crouched children and says, "I'm a giant big and tall, you can't get me, you're too small." Then Goliath freezes and David stands up, says, "I'm David. I'm not afraid!" and throws the newspaper at Goliath. If David hits Goliath, David becomes the new giant and another David is chosen. If the child misses Goliath, new children are chosen to be both David and Goliath. Discuss how God gave David the courage to face Goliath (1 Samuel 17).

15 *Jonah and the Whale*

Start this relay race with the first runners from each team sitting on a pile of pillows (the boat). To get through the course they must do a somersault or roll off of the pillows, and crawl underneath a sheet (held waist high by two people who shake it to simulate waves in the ocean). Finally, they must crawl through a long refrigerator box with a whale painted on the side and then run back to their team and tag the next runner. The first team to have everyone complete the course successfully and be seated at the starting line wins.

16 *Race for the Ark*

Choose one child to be Noah and assign one leader as Noah's assistant. The two of them should walk down a line of the other children and whisper the name of an animal in each child's ear. Be sure that each animal is assigned twice so there will be a pair to board the ark. Then Noah says, "The rain is coming! Hurry and come to the ark!" All the children should then start making their animal sound and walking, crawling, or slithering around trying to find their mate. When a match is found, they head to "the ark" (two chairs with a blanket draped between them) and crawl through the door. Try to see how quickly you can get all the animals safely inside and then serve animal crackers as a reward.

17 *Lion's Den*

One child, chosen as the lion, goes to his den in the center of the circle of other children. With everyone on all fours, have the circle of children say, "Lion, Lion, let's make a deal! Whoever you catch can be your next meal!" Then the lion leaves its den and crawls after the others. Once a child is tagged they must go sit in the lion's den. The last one to be caught is the lion for the next game. It would be scary to be chased by a real lion! But God protected Daniel in the lion's den (Daniel 6:19-22).

18 *Moses, Moses*

Place two jump-ropes on the floor parallel to one another. One child stands between them as Moses and the others line up behind one of the ropes. Children say, "Moses, Moses, may we cross the sea?" Moses responds with, "If you are wearing _____ (color, type of clothing, etc.), you will be safe." All children who fit that description may cross to the other side. Then Moses says, "Soldiers, Soldiers, cross if you dare!" The remaining children try to get to the other side without being tagged by Moses in the middle. Once everyone is caught, Moses can choose another child as a new Moses.

19 *Samuel, Samuel!*

This game will reinforce the truth of the story of Samuel from 1 Samuel 3. One child is chosen to be "Samuel" and lies down with his back to the group and his eyes closed. The leader then taps one child to say this rhyme:

"Samuel, Samuel,
Can you hear?
The Lord your God
is always near."

Samuel then awakens and tries to guess who spoke. When children sit close together it is more challenging to recognize the child speaking. Practice the rhyme several times so that children will be comfortable saying it alone. For younger children the leader might want to simplify the rhyme and simply say, "Samuel, Samuel, I'm calling you."

20 Creation Memory

This game can be used with the story of creation to talk about all the different kinds of animals God created. Find animal stickers or other duplicate animal pictures. Mount two identical pictures on separate cards. It would be wise to laminate these or cover them with clear contact paper. Using five or six pairs of pictures, depending on the age of the children, play the game of "Memory." Cards are turned over, picture face down. Children take turns turning over two pictures, trying to make a match. If they succeed, they can take another turn. The game continues until all the pairs have been matched.

21 Babel Blocks

(Genesis 11)
Build "The Tower of Babel," letting the children take turns adding a block. When the tower falls, count to see how many blocks were used. The leader might want to build the foundation for the tower first, allowing the children to add blocks on top of this foundation. Let the children pretend to talk in different languages. They will enjoy having permission to make noise!

22 *Blinded*

After hearing the story of the blind man, in John 9, children may gain greater understanding of the blind while playing this game. Hide some familiar objects in a large bowl or trash can filled with rice and see if the children can identify them simply by touch. You can blindfold them to keep them from peeking!

23 *Nice Kitty*

This story ties in with the story of Daniel in the lions' den (Daniel 6). Have the group stand in a circle with their hands behind their backs. Choose one player to be Daniel and stand in the center of the circle. The leader walks behind the circle and puts a penny in a player's palm; that player is a kitty.

Any player who is not a kitty is a lion. Daniel walks around the circle, approaches a player, and asks, "Nice kitty?" If a kitty is chosen, the kitty says "Meow," and changes places with Daniel. The leader must now collect and redistribute the pennies. If Daniel chooses a lion, the lion roars, and Daniel must stay in the circle.

24 *Moses in the Bulrushes*

(Exodus 2:1-10)
Select one child to be Moses who stands in the center as the other children join hands and walk in a circle around him. To the tune of, "Farmer in the Dell," have them sing:

"Moses in the Nile,
Watch out for Crocodile.
All the day bulrushes sway,
Moses in the Nile."

"The princess comes along,
The princess comes along,
All the day bulrushes sway,
Moses in the Nile."

Moses selects one child to be the princess. The song continues as "the princess takes a maid," "the maid takes Miriam," and "Miriam takes mother." The children inside the circle then join the circle and the "mother" gets to play the part of Moses and the song begins again.

25 Wooly

Jesus is our Good Shepherd (John 10:1-18). Make two large handprints on poster board and turn them upside down so the fingers become the legs for a lamb and the thumb is the nose. Spread white glue on the palm section of each handprint. Place cotton balls and a pair of salad tongs at the starting line and the lambs on a table ten feet away. At the "go" signal the first person on each of two teams uses the salad tongs to pick up one cotton ball, carry it to their team's lamb, and place it on the glued area. They then return the tongs to the next teammate who repeats the action. The team that covers their lamb with "wool" first wins.

26 Tumbling Walls

Help the children remember the story of the walls of Jericho (Joshua 6:1-27) by playing this game. Divide children into two groups. One group interlocks arms to form the walls of Jericho while the other group marches around "Jericho" seven times, singing as they go (tune of "Ring Around the Rosie"):

"We're marching around Jericho.
Our feet go stomp, our trumpets blow!
Praise God! Praise God!
The walls fall down!"

The "walls" begin to shake and crumble until all children who are the "wall of Jericho" are on the floor. The children change places and play again.

27 Ten Plagues

After studying the plagues of Egypt (Exodus 7—12), play this game so the children can review the story as they work together. Divide the group into teams of five. Assign the name of a different plague to each group, using as many of the ten as you have teams for. Have the children stand around a parachute, holding the edge. (An old sheet will work if a parachute is not available.) Place an inflated beach ball in the center of the parachute. Call the name of one of the plagues and all the children in that group shake the parachute trying to toss the ball off the parachute. In ten or fifteen seconds call a different plague name and then it is that team's turn to try to bounce the ball off the parachute.

28 *Joseph's Coat*

After studying Joseph and his colorful coat (Genesis 37:1-4) play this game to help the children appreciate the story. Paint colored stripes on a sheet to resemble Joseph's coat of many colors and spread it out on the floor. Assign a different point value for each colored stripe. Divide the group into two or more teams, or let the children play as individuals. The children will take turns tossing bean bags onto the coat from five feet away to see how many points they can score.

29 *Feeding the 5,000*

(Matthew 14:14-22)
Divide the group into four or more teams. Have a large bowl filled with fish shaped crackers in the center of the activity. Have the teams spaced evenly around the bowl, with the first person on each team standing ten feet away from the bowl. At the "go" signal the first child on each team will run to the bowl, scoop a spoonful of fish crackers, race back, and drop the fish into their team's basket. The teams will race until all children have gone twice. The team with the most fish crackers wins.

30 *God's the Light*

Play a version of "Red Light, Green Light" by the name of "God's the Light." God's the Light = Green Light and Stop All Sin = Red Light. When all the children reach the game leader, count with the children, "1, 2, 3" (to get their attention) then shout in unison "God's The Light!"

31 *Find It!*

(Luke 15)

All children sit on the floor in a circle and one child is chosen to be the Searcher. The Searcher turns to face away from the circle while another child is chosen to "hide" the lost coin by sitting on it. Then, the Searcher is invited to walk around the outside of the circle while all the other children sing (to the tune of "Farmer in the Dell"):

"Oh, where is your lost coin?
Oh, where is your lost coin?
Search until you find it, now.
Oh, where is your lost coin?"

The children sing louder as the Searcher gets closer to the coin and softer as the Searcher moves further away from the coin. The Searcher uses this clue to guess who is hiding the coin and then pats that child on the head. When the Searcher correctly identifies the child hiding the coin, they exchange places and the child hiding the coin becomes the Searcher. Continue play until everyone has had a chance to be the Searcher.

32 *Telephone Line to Heaven*

Begin by having the children sit in two single-file lines, facing each other. Talk about how the disciples in Acts 1-9 went out and told others the good news about Jesus. Then tell them that each line will receive a message that they must pass on to others, as the disciples did. A leader will whisper the message into the first child's ear and the team must pass the message all the way down the line by whispering the message only once into the next child's ear. The first team to get the message all the way to the end, and have the last person stand and say the message correctly, wins. If neither team gets it correct, the leader can tell everyone the original message and start a new one. Messages should be about the good news of Jesus. ("Jesus died for you!" "Jesus is God's son!" Jesus is alive!")

33 *Catching Fish*

Four children, called fishermen, hold the corners of an old sheet. When the leader says "GO!" the fishermen raise the sheet and then lower it to the ground while the other kids try to run from one side of the sheet to the other without being trapped underneath. When there are only four fish left uncaught, they become the new fishermen. Tell about how Jesus' disciples (in Luke 5) caught more fish than they could hold.

34 *Active Feet*

After teaching the story of the lame man (John 5, Matthew 9, Acts 3), help the children to appreciate their strong legs by playing some relay races. Remind the children frequently that they could not join in if they did not have two strong feet. Sometime during the activity stop and pray, thanking God for healthy bodies.

Suggested relays:
Run, jump, hop, gallop, or march to a boundary line and back.
Crawl like a spider.
Hop with a ball between the legs.
Walk on tiptoe.

35 *The Walls of Jericho*

(Joshua 6)

For this musical game, have all the kids in the group join hands in a circle. In the center of the circle, two kids should hold the corners of a blanket. The leader sings the song below while the children walk in a circle. Children can join in as they learn the words:

(TUNE: "POP GOES THE WEASEL")
The walls are high in Je-ri-cho
How can we make it over?
We asked God to show us the way
And this is what He told us.

March round 'n' round the city walls
March round a count of se-ven.
And when we all began to shout . . .
Crash! (children give a loud clap)
The walls came tumbling do-wn!

"1 . . . 2 . . . 3 . . . 4 . . . 5 . . . 6 . . . 7 . . . !"

When the song says "CRASH" the two kids holding the blanket in the center put it on the ground and everyone will rush to find a place to sit down by the count of seven. The last two to be seated on the blanket must hold the blanket for the next round. As the kids become more comfortable with the game and more familiar with the words to the song, encourage them to sing it along with you. The children will also enjoy making the clap on "Crash!" as loud as possible.

36 *Storm!*

This group activity can be used to simulate the events of Matthew 8, when Jesus calmed the storm. (This story is also found in Mark 4 and Luke 8.) Place a sheet in an open part of the room. Instruct the children in your group to find a place around the sheet to hold on to. Once everyone has a spot that they can hold onto with both hands, tell the children to drop to their knees and kneel next to the sheet—but don't let go of the sheet. Place a beach ball on the sheet and have children move the "water" (sheet) slowly, watching the "boat" (ball) gently move. Then, make the waves higher by moving the sheet more vigorously—with the goal of keeping the ball on the sheet. When the leader whispers, "Jesus said, 'Be still,' " the children stop moving the sheet and make the sea calm again. You can repeat this a number of times, varying the amount of time the kids have to move the water before you instruct them to make it still. Once the children have mastered this activity on their knees, have them try it standing up.

37 *Colorful Coat Toss-Up*

In advance: Stuff a paper bag with newspaper or tissue paper, so it is full but not too heavy. Tape the end of the bag securely. Next, take many colors of markers and draw all over the bag, to symbolize the many colors that were in Joseph's coat.

Have the group stand in a circle. Tell the children that the objective of this game is to see how long the group can cooperate and keep the bag in the air by taking turns tossing it up. The kids can move into the circle once the game starts in order to catch the "coat" but encourage them to stay in their own area so that children in all parts of the circle have a chance to play. The children can bump the bag back up into the air if they want to, but it is probably easiest to have the children catch the bag and then throw it back into the air. Practice this for a while and then have the kids count as a group to see how many times in a row they can throw the bag and catch it without it touching the floor. An optional way to play this is to paint the bag with glow-in-the-dark paints or put glow-in-the-dark tape on it so that you can turn out the lights and have kids play in the dark.

38 *Noah's Ark*

(Genesis 6:1—9:1)
Give a feel for what life on Noah's Ark might have been like with this game. Make a masking tape ark shape on the floor. Group the children into pairs and assign a different animal to each pair. Let them sit in the "ark" to listen to the story, giving each animal pair a "stall." After the story is over, have the children think of the sound and motion that their animal pair makes. Then the leader calls

the names of the animals. When each pair hears their animal name called, they make their sound and motion. Start off calling out the names slowly so that the children can get used to hearing their animal names and responding. Then start to call the names of the animals faster and faster so they have to listen carefully for their turn to "speak." When one pair of animals forgets to "speak" they leave the ark and sit around the edge of it to help listen for others who might miss their call. Continue playing, giving the animals different instructions for each round. (Instructions could include things such as: make your animal sounds very softly, make your animal motions very large, or very small, etc.) The last animal pair that is left in the "ark" wins the game.

BIBLE TIMES

39 *Fill Up the Jar*

Explain to the children that beans and lentils were common foods in Bible-times. Place a big container of beans and lentils on the floor and an empty cooking pot a few yards away. Announce that the whole class is going to see how much of the pot they can fill in two minutes. Give each child a small cup and demonstrate how they will scoop the beans into their cup, carry them to the pot, pour them in, and go back for more. Now, set the timer, and let the fun begin!

40 *Oil for My Lamp*

Tell the children about oil lamps that were used for household lighting during Bible times. The children can pretend their paper cups are the lamps, and the water is the oil. Have each child fill their "lamp" half full, and then race from a start to finish line. The winner is the first to get across the line without spilling any water. If anyone spills all of their water, their lamp is out of oil and they must close their eyes and walk in darkness across the finish line. (You may want to spread a tarp or sheet on the floor to catch any spills.)

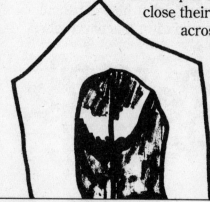

41 *Donkey Relay*

Discuss with your group that animals were used for transportation in Bible times and it was the rider's responsibility to make sure the animal had food and drink to survive long, hot trips. Divide the group into two equal teams and have each child find a partner. One child begins the race as the donkey, and the other as the rider. When the leader says, "Go!" the donkey, with rider on back, crawls as fast as possible to a plastic pitcher of water at the other side of the room. Here the rider must get off the donkey, fill a portion of a cup with water, serve the water to the donkey, and then get down on all fours. The new rider hops on and the pair races back to the starting point. The rider now gets off the donkey and feeds it a carrot or apple slice, signaling the next pair in line to go. The first team to have everyone finished and seated wins.

42 *The Lost Sheep*

Children sit in a circle with one child, selected to be the shepherd, seated in the middle. While the shepherd's eyes are closed, the leader will give a little piece of wool (cotton ball) to one of the children. Explain that the wool represents a lost sheep and that in Bible times a shepherd watched his sheep carefully to make sure none of them got lost or hurt. Once the wool is safely hidden behind the child's back, the whole group says, "Shepherd, shep-

herd, where is your sheep?" The shepherd can now look around and guess who has the wool. Once the sheep is found, that child becomes the new shepherd.

43 Taking a Trip

Talk with the children about how Jesus and his disciples traveled many places. They didn't have cars or airplanes, so most of the time they walked. Go on a walking journey around the room together by placing cards in a box that have instructions written on them such as, walk to the window, turn around, take two steps backward. All the kids should stand in a group around the leader and take turns drawing a card from the box. The leader reads the card and the whole group follows the instructions together.

44 Gone Fishing

Children sit on the floor in a row with hands in back of them. They are fish. One child, chosen to be the fisherman, sits facing the fish. Explain that the fisherman is looking for a treasure (a bag of fish crackers), but the fish are hiding it. The fisherman covers his eyes while the leader places the treasure in the hands of a fish. The fisherman uncovers his eyes when the leader says "PASS!" The treasure is passed from one fish to another (behind their backs) in either direction. The leader says "STOP!" and the passing of the treasure stops. The fisherman tries to name the player who has the bag. At the end, share fish crackers with the children. (Fresh ones may be needed to replace crushed ones from the bag!) While the kids eat, talk about how people who lived in the time of Jesus fished as their job.

45 *Let's Catch Fish*

This is a simulation game about the livelihood of fishermen in Bible-times.

The leader can arrange two sheets in different areas to represent nets like the ones mentioned in Luke 5:4. The nets trapped fish like a huge bag in the water. Divide the class into two teams and choose one child from each team to throw fish (3" x 5" cards). All the other members of the team must hold the sides of the sheet and work together to catch the fish as they are thrown. Each team then pulls their "fish catch" to an imaginary boat. The team who brings in the most fish wins.

46 *Pass the Crown*

The Bible is full of kings and queens, both good ones who obeyed God and others who did not. For this game the children will pass a crown around the circle from head to head. As long as it is moving, it is the crown of a good king or queen but when the leader rings a bell, the crown stops and the child who has the crown is out. The game continues until only one child is left.

47 *Journey by Foot*

How far have you walked in your life? Well, the Israelites walked for years! In fact, many people in the Bible walked a lot. During this "journey by foot" obstacle course, time the kids and see who can get through it the fastest. Use what you have in the room to make the obstacle course. Some suggestions: crawl under a table, step over shoe boxes, walk through plastic bowling pins without knocking them over, eat a cracker, drink some water, and crawl through a box backward.

48 *Run, Donkey, Run*

Divide the group into teams and have team members pair up. Give each pair a length of yarn or string. At the signal, the first pair each takes an end of the string and stretches it between them. With one as the "front legs" and one as the "back legs," the two children gallop around a chair at the other end of the playing area, then back to the line. When tagged, the next pair can go.

49 *Carpenter's Workshop*

Give each team of kids a pile of screws and nuts. Set a timer for two minutes and see how many they can get put together in that amount of time. The team that gets the most wins. Although he didn't use the modern supplies of screws and nuts, Jesus' father was a carpenter. Talk with the kids about ways Jesus might have helped his father in the workshop.

50 *Into the Fold*

Explain to the children that shepherds in the Bible had to protect their sheep. Every night they brought them into the fold where they were protected from wild animals. Play a game of crawling tag where some children kneel together in a semi-circle to make a fold, one child is the wolf, and the others are sheep. The wolf chases the sheep (with everyone down on all fours) but cannot tag any sheep while they are inside the fold.

51 *Oh, Great King!*

In the days of some Bible characters, such as Esther, the kings were very powerful. No one could even see the king unless he allowed it. If you went to see a king without being invited, he could have you killed, unless he extended the end of his golden scepter and accepted you. Play a version of "Mother May I" called, "Oh, Great King." One child, chosen to be the king, stands in front of the group and is given something that represents the golden scepter. Each child in their turn says, "Oh, Great King, may I _____?" (some action, such as take two steps forward). The King says nothing but extends the scepter if that child can take the requested action. If the scepter is not extended, the child cannot move on that turn.

52 *Sheep, Sheep, Shepherd*

The Bible is full of stories about sheep and shepherds! Have the children play a variation on "Duck, Duck, Goose." Play just like the original game, except have the children say, "Sheep, Sheep, Shepherd!"

53 *Battle of the Cotton Balls*

During the times recorded in the Old Testament, there were many great battles in which God protected and gave victory to His people. Have the children participate in their own battle with cotton balls. Divide the children into two teams and assign them to opposite sides of the room. Mark a middle line on the floor with masking tape. Distribute cotton balls to each child and tell them that they are to throw the cotton balls across the line, trying to hit a member of the other team. They may go as close to the middle line as they like but cannot cross it. Children should keep track of how many of their own cotton balls strike the enemy, but a child is not out if he or she is hit. Cotton balls that are thrown can be picked up and used again.

FAMILY FUN

54 Favorite Family Fun

Rehearse with the children ideas of fun family activities, such as picnicking or hiking. After the children share some of their own ideas, tell the children they get to act out the activity ideas any way they wish to when the leader calls out one of the suggestions. For instance, if the leader calls out "horseback riding!" the children can pretend to climb on a horse, brush a horse, feed a carrot to a horse, etc. If the leader calls out "Family freeze!" all the children should freeze right in their tracks; children who move during the freeze time are out.

55 Helpers at Home

In advance: In two separate areas, scatter an even number of children's books and toys. Divide the class into two teams. Tell the children that once the leader says to go, they should all work together to 1) stack the books in one cardboard box, 2) stack the toys in the other cardboard box, 3) have all their team members sit down around their team's boxes. Let the children know that even if their team isn't the fastest in the game, they can still help their family at home by picking up their toys.

56 Busy Families

This game is similar to "Squirrels in the Trees" and may help children to appreciate the work their parents do for them. Divide children into groups of three. In each group designate one to be the mother, one the father, and the third the baby. The mother and father join hands to form a house. The baby sits inside the house. The leader will call out sentences such as, "Father cuts the grass," "Mother goes to work," "Mother washes our clothes," "Father cooks our meals," "Baby crawls away." Each time mother, father, or baby is mentioned, they exchange places with another mother, father, or baby. If there are one or two extra children, they can be babies also. Several families can have twins!

57 Family Circle

This game helps preschoolers identify the roles of boys and girls in families as brothers, sisters, mothers and fathers. Instruct children to sit in a circle. Choose one child to walk around the outside of the circle tapping each child on the head. The child says "sister" each time a girl is tapped and "brother" each time a boy is tapped until he chooses someone to chase him around the circle by yelling "Mom!" or "Dad!" This mom or dad chases the child around the circle and back to the original starting point. Then the child joins the Family Circle and the mom/dad becomes the child who taps the other kids in the circle.

58 *Food Tour*

Children follow the leader on an imaginary tour based on something that people in their family do for them. The leader and children can make the motions together. Ideas for tours could include chores around the house or going to work. A tour of the grocery store where parents shop for food might go something like this:

"Let's take a tour of the grocery store to see some of the wonderful foods our parents make for us. Brr! When the door opens, feel that air conditioning. (Shiver, shiver.) The manager of the store said we could sample anything we like. Yum! Yum! (Rub stomach.) Let's start here in the fruits and vegetables. Mmm. Here's a ripe banana. (Peel and eat banana.) Here's some crunchy celery. (Take a big crunchy bite.) Hey! I love corn on the cob, don't you? (Eat corn.) God sure thought of a lot of interesting foods. Isn't it wonderful that we have parents who buy and prepare our food, and families to eat with? What foods do you see?"

59 *Family Statues*

Play some music while the kids act out their favorite activity to do with their family. When the music stops, all the children freeze. The leader then tries to guess what different children are doing. After guessing a few, turn the music back on and continue with the game, guessing activities of different children each time.

60 *Family Sand Sketch*

Fill disposable aluminum pie pans with sand and water. Have the children sit on a tarp and give each child one pan. Ask them to use their fingers to sketch a picture in the sand of a member of their family. Then ask the children to erase their pictures by running their hands over the sand. Continue in this way, giving the children things to sketch in the sand. Include things such as different members of their family, their pets, their house, their yard, their favorite toy, etc. For variety, divide the children into pairs or have them choose partners. Each child's partner must try to guess what the other child is sketching in his or her sand. The children can alternate sketching and guessing with their partners.

61 *Gather the Family*

On several index cards, draw stick figures to represent members of the family. (Skirt on mom, tie on dad, ponytails for girl, short hair for boy, baby, grandpa with beard, grandma with bun in hair.) Make enough of each card that the children can have one for each person in their real family. Show the cards to the children and explain to them what family member each card stands for. Place the cards in various boxes around the room. Have at least one box for each different family member card. At the signal, each child must gather a card for each member in their family. Make sure that the children know that their card collection will not be the same as others because everyone's families are different. Once the children have collected a card that represents each person in their family, they should sit down and raise their cards in the air. Once all the children are finished, take volunteers to come to the front of the group to show their cards and tell the names of the people in their family. Have some extra cards on hand in case a child is missing a card when they describe their family to the group.

62 *Baby Games*

This game helps to build appreciation for babies and understanding of what is involved for a family to take care of one. Set up a circle of chairs in advance and make small signs to tape to most of the chairs. Each sign should have a symbol related to baby care. For example, draw a rubber duck for bath time, or a rattle for play time, a bottle for meals, or a diaper for changing time. Tell the children to walk around the circle and then sit in a chair as soon as they hear the leader say "BABY." If the chair they sit in has a symbol on it, the children can act it out. Those children who do not have symbols attached to their chairs can act out a baby crawling. The children should walk (or crawl) around the circle, acting out their symbol until they hear the leader say "BABY" again. When they hear this, they should go to a new chair and sit in it. Now they will have new symbols to act out for this round. Because no one gets out in this game, there should be enough chairs for all the children on each round. When you are finished playing this game, let the children tell their own experiences with babies and why they think babies are special.

63 *Family Wrap*

Divide the children into groups of five. Give each group one roll of toilet paper to work with. Instruct the kids that they are to make costumes out of the toilet paper to dress three kids in their group. They must dress these three people in their group to look like a mother, a father, and a son or a daughter. When the children have finished creating their toilet paper costumes, allow each team to model their family for the whole group and explain what costumes they created with the toilet paper. They can also explain why they think it makes the child look like the member of the family that he or she represents. If you have more time, let the children switch places so that the kids who designed the clothes last time get to be dressed up. Assign different family members (aunts, uncles, grandparents, etc.) this time and let the children model the new outfits when they are completed.

ALL ABOUT CHURCH

64 *Church-Time Fun*

Divide the class into three teams. During this relay race, have the children carry a penny in a paper cup and sit down in a chair halfway to the finish line. While seated in the chair, have the children sing the chorus of "Jesus Loves Me," and run the remaining distance from the chair to the finish line. Finally, they can deposit a penny in a box to simulate an offering collection and then run back to their teammates. Have each child take turns repeating the same actions until each child has finished. See which team is done first.

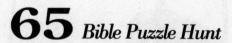

65 *Bible Puzzle Hunt*

Reading and learning Bible verses is an important part of going to church, and this is a fun way to do it! Write out a verse putting only one word on each index card. Place the cards end to end and cut matching shapes so the cards fit together like a puzzle. Hide the cards around the room and let the children search for them. Once they have all the cards they can all work to fit the puzzle pieces together. Once the puzzle is complete, have a leader read the verse out loud and the kids repeat it.

66 *Musical Prayer*

Write numbers on masking tape and place them on the floor in a circle. Each child stands on a number and then the whole group moves around the circle while singing, "Jesus Loves Me." At the end of the song each child should be standing on a new number. The leader then calls out a number and that child shares one thing he or she is thankful for. After a few children have shared, the leader will say a prayer thanking God for the things mentioned. Repeat as many times as desired!

67 *Popcorn*

Children will find that reviewing Bible verses in church is fun with the following activity: Children may sit in a circle or a straight line. Designate one child to begin the Bible verse by "popping up" and saying the first word. The next child "pops up" with the second word. Each child continues with the next word. Repeat the verse until all have had an opportunity to participate. Afterwards, reward them with a popcorn treat.

68 Going to Church

Help kids make up motions to this fun song (to the tune of "Here We Go 'Round the Mulberry Bush") as they learn to understand and appreciate their time in church.

Suggested verses:
This is the way we go to church,
Go to church, go to church,
This is the way we go to church,
On a Sunday morning.

This is the way we greet our friends.
This is the way we read God's word.
This is the way we close our eyes.
This is the way we say our prayers.
This is the way we give our gifts.
This is the way we listen well.
This is the way we sing to God.
This is the way we say good bye.

69 Musical Plates

Begin the game by putting a paper plate on the floor for each child. Turn on some Bible songs that the kids will enjoy hearing and learning. Instruct the children to move, sing, and clap. When the music stops, each child should walk to a plate and stand on it. When the music begins again, the children should leave their plates and return to what they were doing. Continue to play like musical chairs, removing one plate each time. The kids who are "out" can still enjoy the music and can help the leader by choosing which plates to take out.

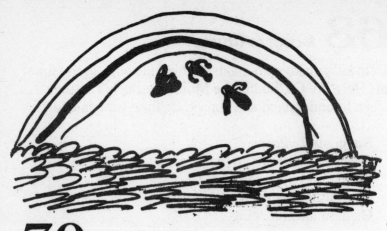

70 *Boom, Boom, Clang, Clang*

One important way of praising God in church is through music. Sometimes music makes you want to jump, shout, and sing! Create a joyful band to make music for God by giving the children various instruments (or let kids make the instrument sounds themselves). The leader conducts a parade around the room, weaving here and there and calling out the names of instruments. Children with those instruments join the parade and start making a joyful noise to the Lord. The leader can also give instructions to skip, jump, and spin around.

71 *The Working Church*

Everyone in the church is important and has special talents and jobs. Help the kids see some of the different people in the church and how important each person is by acting out these roles of people in the church. Have the kids can repeat the actions and words after the leader. When you finish acting out all the roles, see if the kids can think of any other people in the church. Help the kids make up actions to show what their jobs are.

Pastor: *(holding an imaginary book)* "This is what the Bible says."

Choir member: *(sings)* "La-la-la!"

Janitor: *(singing and sweeping)* "This is the way we sweep the church."

Receptionist: *(answering a phone)* "Hello, may I help you?"

Kid: *(singing)* "Jesus loves me, this I know."

Nursery worker: *(cradling an imaginary baby)* "There, there, little baby."

Sunday school teacher: *(opening an imaginary Bible)* "Who knows today's memory verse?"

Music director/choir leader: *(Opens an imaginary song book)* "Let's all praise God together."

72 *Going to Church*

Going to church can be a fun thing to do . . . especially with a friend. Choose two children to form the church door by clasping hands and raising their arms. All the other children move single-file through the door as they sing (to the tune of "London Bridge"):

How I love to go to church,
Go to church, go to church.
How I love to go to church.
Won't you come with me?

When the song ends, the two children forming the church door drop their arms and trap the child standing between them. The child caught standing in the "door" when the song ends then chooses a partner to form a new door. Once the new church door is in place, the children begin walking through it, singing the song, and the whole game repeats.

73 *Stop the Music*

Describe to the children the many kinds of movement they can make about the church (see below). While the music is playing, have children move about without touching each other. But when the music stops have them "Freeze" in their spots. Let each child tell you what they are doing. Then, start the music again!

(Suggested movement themes:)
Singing hymns or praise songs
Praying
Reading the Bible
Directing the choir
Preaching or teaching

74 *Take It to the Box*

In advance: make slips of paper that are designed to look like dollar bills. You may want to make them resemble different bills or just design them to look like play paper money in general. Hide these slips of paper money around the room. Show the children an example of the paper money. Tell the children that they will be playing a game that has to do with offering—bringing our money to God. Tell the kids that you have hidden paper money (like the piece you are holding) around the room. They will have a certain amount of time and in that time they are to try to find as much money as possible. When all the bills are found or when time is up, have the children bring their bills to the front of the room and put them in an offering box. Make sure that every child has something to put in the box. (You may need to have a few spare "bills" in case some of the children don't find any on their own.) To play again, choose a couple of kids to help you hide the "money" and then have the rest of the group begin the search again.

75 *Church Formation*

Divide the children into two teams. Instruct them to build a church building out of their own bodies. The children should work together to figure out what the building should look like and decide how they can fit all their team members together to form that shape. Then they should all lie down on the floor so that their whole team forms the shape of a church building. For younger children, you may want to bring in a simple line-drawing of a church so they have an idea of what their formation should look like. They may also need the help of an adult to visualize what the finished church should look like and to help them decide who should go where. Be available to help the kids but try to let them figure it out on their own first. The important thing is that they get involved and have fun, not that they create a perfect finished product! Remind the kids that even though real church buildings are usually made out of bricks, wood, or stone, the church really is the people!

CHARACTER BUILDERS

76 *Let Your Light Shine*

This small group game gets children working together using flashlights—symbolizing the light we share as Christians. Before the game begins, make two large circles on the floor with masking tape. Give each child a flashlight. Break the group up into two small teams. Explain that each team should try to focus their individual flashlight beam with the others on their team so the combined flashlights make one large light. (You may need to demonstrate.) Tell the children that the first team to focus their lights together and trace their circle on the floor with the combined beam, wins.

77 *Strong and Courageous*

We often have to do things that we are scared of but God can help us have the courage to do them. David is a good example of courage as he faced the lions and bears to protect his father's sheep (1 Samuel 17:33-37). Emphasize the fact that it was only with the Lord's help that David had the courage to do what he did. In this game, based on the courage that David showed, have the children line up and take turns throwing a table tennis ball, with sticky Velcro strips on it, at a felt picture of a lion or a bear. Cheer for the children as they try to protect their sheep from these animals.

78 *Friends Help Each Other*

This game focuses on the concept of friends helping each other. Select pairs of children to work as partners and give each pair a heart cut out of red construction paper. Explain to the children that they both need to hold onto the paper heart, start out from the common starting line, and try to be the first pair to go across the finish line with their paper heart still intact. They must help each other to move quickly without tearing the heart. (But if everyone tears their heart, find out which child's heart is torn the least.)

79 *Let's Work Together*

Bring in various objects that come in pairs and have the group identify them together. (Examples: sock and shoe, plate and napkin, crayon and paper, book and bookmark, etc.) Then take the objects and scatter them throughout the room. Each child should find a partner and hold a paper bag between the two of them. Then they must walk together around the room and find pairs of objects that go together. Each child must pick up one of the objects and when both are found, they can put them in the bag together. The first partners to find three pairs of objects yell, "Friends!" Those children sit down until the other partners have found three pairs of objects or all the objects have been collected. Talk about how each set of partners had to work together and how working together can help us be better friends.

80 Blind Thankfulness

Half the kids create a maze by crouching down to become rocks to go around, forming arches with their arms to go under, and kneeling with their arms extended to make logs to step over. Have the other half of the group pair off with one partner being blind and the other the leader. Have the partners go all the way through the maze and then switch places. The goal is not to be the fastest but to lead your partner safely through the maze. How thankful we should be for the friends that help us and for good eyes that can see!

81 Air Ball

Mark a starting line and a finish line on the floor using masking tape. Give each child a table-tennis ball and have kids line up behind the starting line. Explain to the children that they should place their ball on the floor, kneel behind their ball, then gently blow it toward the finish line. Play against the clock, with children playing several times and trying to beat their previous time record. Talk about the importance of perseverance and sticking with something even when it is hard.

82 *Hug Parade*

This version of "London Bridge" gives children a chance to show God's love to others. Have one child join hands with you to create an arch. Have the other children parade under the arch as you sing this song to the tune of "London Bridge."

> God wants us to show our love,
> Show our love,
> Show our love.
> God wants us to show our love,
> To each other.

On the word "other," drop your arms around the child who is under the arch. Together with the child holding your hands, hug the child in the middle. Then let this child join hands with you to create the arch and play again. Continue playing until each child has been hugged at least once!

83 *Wonderfully Made*

To encourage self-esteem and to teach the truth of Psalm 139:14. ("I am . . . wonderfully made.") introduce the following game:

Children stand in a circle and one child begins by saying, "I am wonderfully made. I can _____." He fills in the blank with such words as "jump," "laugh," or "crawl." The rest of the children join in doing what the child says. Go around the circle, allowing each child to have a turn. At the end, see if the group can name all of the activities and do them in order.

84 *Heaped in a Hoop*

Begin by laying some large plastic hoops around the room. (Start with one for each child if possible. Otherwise assign a certain number of children who can be in a hoop to begin with.) Play some music and have the children walk around the hoops, but tell them not to touch any of them while the music is playing. When the music stops, each child steps into the nearest hoop. There should be enough hoops for every child. Once everyone has found a hoop, the leader chooses a hoop to take out of play. The leader removes the hoop and then starts the music again. The game continues as before and each time the music stops, children must step into the nearest hoop. No one is ever out in this game because as hoops are removed, there can be more than one child in each hoop. Play until there are only one or two hoops left. Encourage the kids to help each other find room for every child inside these two hoops. It is quite crowded with all those kids heaped in a hoop—but fun too! Then, without music, see if you can fit everyone in your group into one hoop.

85 Finder's Keepers

This game helps children develop good teamwork skills. Divide the group into teams. Have each team choose a "finder." Together (with a leader), the players and finders determine a special call they will use to identify themselves—perhaps a "beep" or a "clap" or an "eek!" Calls should only be one syllable. Once each team's call is decided, the finders turn their backs or leave the room while all the other players hide. When the finders return, have all the lights turned off. At the signal, the finders try to find their fellow team members by listening for the special calls. The children who are hiding should try to make it easy to be found by repeating their team's special call over and over again. When a finder locates a person on his or her team, the finder places his or her hand on the child's head and makes the team's special call. The child who has been found answers with the call and then goes to sit in a designated area for that team. If the child is from a different team and answers with a different call, the finder should leave that child alone and go on to find someone from his or her own team. The first team to have everyone found by the finder and to be seated all together in their area wins.

86 Who's Got My Galoshes?

Divide the group into teams. Put enough pairs of shoes and boots in a pile so there is one pair for each child. At the signal, the first child in each line runs to the pile and tries to find a matching pair of shoes. Children remove their own shoes and add them to the pile, then put on the new pair and run to tag the next child in line. The first team to have all players back in line in new shoes wins, but continue the game until all team members on all teams have played. Now play again—the object being that everyone finds their own shoes. No one can win on their own—the whole team must work together to win!

87 Gentleness Grab Bag

Place a number of objects that have to be handled with gentleness into paper bags. Items could include an egg, a water balloon, a baby doll, etc. Have children take turns coming up and putting their hands inside the bags. Without seeing what is inside, see if they can guess what the objects are. To make this a competitive game, divide the kids into teams and see which team can correctly identify the most objects.

88 Cooperation

Have each child select a partner and then divide the group into four teams. Assign each team a color—this will be the color of their team's balloons. The first set of partners on each team will be given one table-tennis paddle each. Place a balloon between the paddles. Each partner must put enough pressure on the paddle to secure the balloon long enough to carry it to a box ten feet away. When the partners have successfully placed their balloon in the box, they run back, give the paddles to the next set of partners on their team, and play continues. If a pair drops a balloon, they are disqualified, and they must take the paddles to the next pair in line. When everyone else has gone, the pairs that dropped their balloons get one more chance to take their balloon to the box. The team that has the most balloons in the box when all teams have completed the exercise is the winner.

89 *Pass It On!*

Divide the class in half and seat them on the floor in two circles, back to back (one facing in and the other facing out). Instruct each circle to pass a ball or bean bag around the circle as they sing (to the tune of "Mary Had a Little Lamb"):

I know Jesus loves us so,
Loves us so, loves us so.
I know Jesus loves us so,
And I will pass it on!

Each time the verse ends, the two children holding the ball or bean bag exchange places.

HAPPY HOLIDAYS

90 Christmas Angel Action

The excitement of Jesus' birth can be relived through remembering the host of angels which heralded the occasion. Play a version of "Pin the Tail on the Donkey." Have the children pin angel pictures on top of a picture of a Christmas tree.

91 Fill the Manger

Have three teams of children line up behind starting marks. Explain what a manger is and that a manger was Jesus' first bed. Tell the children that each team is responsible for transporting the straw (or shredded paper) to their team's box, simulating the real manger Jesus slept in. The first team that can successfully transport every piece of straw or paper to fill their box wins the competition.

92 *Hide the Easter Eggs*

This game helps children to learn a Bible verse related to Easter. Write out the Bible verse Matthew 28:20, "... I, Jesus, am with you always ..." (one word for each piece of paper.)

Associate each word with an illustration from a pictorial sequence of a flower growing (ground, seed, sprout, bud, leaf, flower). Insert each word in a plastic egg. Each team will have the same verse hidden in their team's eggs and each team's eggs will be a different color. The leader hides the eggs for each team. The team that can find all the eggs, unscramble the verse, and put the verse together in correct order according to the plant sequence pictures, wins. Since the children won't be able to read, they will put it together according to the flower pictures and then a leader can read the verse at the end.

93 *Follow the Star*

This game goes with the story of the Wise Men who followed the star of Bethlehem. Cut out star shapes from the two different colors of construction paper. Tape the stars (at least twenty for each team) around an area for children to find them. Divide the class into teams. Assign one of the star colors to each team. Set the timer for one minute. Explain to the children that the team that finds the most stars for their team during the time limit wins. Hide the stars in new places and play again.

94 Secret Picture Card Game

Use this game to review or tell the Easter story. Divide the children into groups of two to three and give each group one card. The cards should each have a picture of something that relates to the story (three crosses, the large rock in front of the tomb, an angel, etc.) Once the groups have their card, let them talk together to make sure they all agree on what it is. Then one member from each group comes to the front and holds the card so the rest cannot see it. The large group tries to guess what the secret picture is by asking yes or no questions. Once all the cards have been guessed, have the group work together to put them in order of how the story really happened.

95 Candy Canes

Use this game to bring significance to a Christmas symbol. Tell the children this candy cane story: It was first made by a candy maker in England many years ago. He wanted children to think about Jesus' birthday so he made the candy cane as a reminder. The three red stripes remind us of the Father, Son, and Holy Spirit. The wider stripe stands for Jesus. White is for His purity, red for His blood. It looks like a shepherd's staff. Upside down, it is a "J." Hide candy canes in the room and let the children hunt for them. If you have a tree in the room, the children can add some as decorations.

96 *Musical Hearts*

This game may be used for Valentine's Day as a reminder of God's love.

This game is a reversed version of "Musical Chairs." Place two hearts cut from poster board on the floor in a large circle. Write "God is love" or "Jesus loves me" on each heart. Begin with one child walking around the hearts while the music plays. When the music stops, that child stands on a heart and any other child can go and stand on the second heart. Add a heart each time until all the children are standing on hearts. Talk with the kids about how God's love is big enough for all of us.

97 *Holiday Hustle*

This game uses good listening skills and helps kids learn certain things that are associated with Christian holidays. Establish two boundary lines (indoors or outdoors) far enough apart so that children can run from one to the other. Have the children line up on one boundary line. The leader should stand behind the children and the boundary line. The leader tells the children what holiday name to listen for, such as Easter. The leader calls out words of things that are typically associated with that holiday (empty tomb, cross, new life, stone rolled away). The children should stay on the boundary line until they hear the leader say the actual holiday name. When the holiday name is called the children run to the other boundary and the leader chases them. Any children who are caught must freeze and stand where they were tagged. They must stand there frozen until they hear the leader call the name of the next holiday. The child can then run from his or her frozen spot to the boundary line that the other children are running toward. It's best to do mostly chasing with just enough catching to make it a fun and exciting challenge for the kids.

98 *Holiday Bowling*

Decorate (or have the children decorate) some plastic or paper cups for whatever holiday you are celebrating. You may want to use stickers and already made holiday pictures or let the children simply color the cups with colors that are associated with a particular holiday (green and red for Christmas, pastels for Easter, etc.). Mark a fairly wide bowling lane on the floor using masking tape. On the floor, at the very end of the bowling lane, set up the decorated holiday cups in a formation like bowling pins. Then let the children use a tennis ball or soft indoor ball to bowl. Let the children rotate, taking turns knocking over the cups and setting them up again for the next player. You can designate stations so that there is always one child bowling, one child setting up the pins and one child who is in charge of retrieving the ball and returning it to the next child in line to bowl. If you have a large group, set up more than one bowling lane so that the children can be an active part of holiday bowling the whole time.

99 *Holiday Concentration*

Draw holiday symbols on 3" x 5" index cards. Be sure there are two identical cards of each symbol. Lay the cards upside down, in rows, on the floor. Play like "Concentration," where the children take turns trying to turn over two cards that match. The first child turns over two cards. If they match, he or she gets to keep them and that child gets to choose two cards to turn over again. If the two cards do not match, that child must turn both cards back over and the next child gets to take a turn. The children can only turn over two cards each time, and the child with the most pairs at the end is the winner!

100 *Snowman Race*

Have each child make a snowman out of marshmallows, following these instructions: Use a toothpick as the center for the bodies and stick it through the middle of two large marshmallows. Then stick a toothpick out either side of the top marshmallow of the snowman and attach small marshmallows to the toothpicks to form arms. Let the children draw faces on their marshmallow snowmen using fine-tipped markers. Then have a snowman race! Place some books under two cookie sheets to prop them up side-by-side. They should be the same size and should slope down at the same angle. The angle should be fairly steep so that the snowmen will slide down without getting stuck. Have the children form two lines behind the cookie sheets. As each child gets to the "sledding hills" he or she will place the snowman at the top of the "hill." The child must wait for the snowman from the child in the other line to be ready and then the leader says, "Go!" The two children then let go of their snowmen and see which makes it to the bottom of the hill first. After everyone has